IN OLD PHOTO

BRITA

C000054089

BRAINTREE

PAST & PRESENT

JOHN MARRIAGE

SUTTON PUBLISHING

Sutton Publishing Limited
Phoenix Mill · Thrupp · Stroud
Gloucestershire · GL5 2BU

First published 2003

Copyright © John Marriage, 2003

Title page photograph: High Street,
Braintree.

British Library Cataloguing in Publication Data
A catalogue record for this book is available from the
British Library.

ISBN 0-7509-3157-4

Typeset in 10.5/13.5 Photina.
Typesetting and origination by
Sutton Publishing Limited.
Printed and bound in England by
J.H. Haynes & Co. Ltd, Sparkford.

*Dedicated to Charles Edward and Daisy
Rosetta Harris and their thirteen children*

A copy of an engraving showing the High Street, looking towards Chelmsford, *c.* 1850.

CONTENTS

White Hart corner from Bank Street.

INTRODUCTION

Braintree and Bocking were once two entirely separate villages but have long since fused into a single town. At quite an early date the built-up area extended over the two separate civil parishes. However, the first known settlement in the vicinity was on a defensive position on the ridge between the rivers Brain and Pant, at that point only a mile apart where there was a crossing of the east–west orientated Stane Street with another Roman road from Chelmsford (*Caesaromagus*) towards the north-east. In Roman times Stane Street was of considerable importance as it ran between Colchester (*Camulodunum*), initially the capital of Roman England, and St Albans (*Verulanium*), as well as to Watling Street and Ermine Street, two of the great national routes from London (*Londinium*) to the provinces. Although of lesser importance the route through Chelmsford was also well used, as it gave direct access from London northwards via a settlement at Long Melford to East Anglia.

Before the Romans came Braintree was the site of an Iron Age settlement, and until fairly recently traces of earthworks belonging to that era survived in the grounds of Mount House. During the Roman period a small community developed at the intersection of the two roads, but their site was probably abandoned when the Romans left, and the history of Braintree really began in 1199 when the Bishop of London established a small trading town close to the intersection of the two roads simultaneously with others at Chelmsford, Bishops Stortford and elsewhere. Some authorities have suggested from the topography that the bishop intended to reproduce an identical ground plan to that of Chelmsford and, indeed, there are many similarities, even though the site lacks the proximity of a river as in his other communities. Bocking grew up along the Sudbury Road, where even now in Bradford Street there are very fine medieval houses. Its special assets were the weirs and mills of the River Pant (upper Blackwater).

The name Braintree originally referred only to the Bishop of London's little community and was at first only a minor part of the manor of Great Rayne, owned by the bishop. The centre of the latter, which included an episcopal palace and grange, was a mile to the south-east of the present town centre, at what is now Chapel Hill. Traces of these ancient structures existed until the nineteenth century but disappeared under factories and warehouses, now themselves replaced.

Throughout the medieval period and middle ages Braintree was an important stopover for travellers from the Midlands proceeding via Harwich to the Low

Countries, as well as pilgrims from southern England on their way to the shrines at Bury St Edmunds and at Walsingham, though this activity was reduced by the Reformation. The town suffered a major setback in 1665 when the Black Death visited the area and a third of the population died.

Weaving, in the form of broadcloth, was first established in the fourteenth century and was augmented by Flemish émigrés who settled here after fleeing the Low Countries following religious persecution. Their cloth became known as 'Bockings'. Later George Courtauld, himself descended from Huguenots, moved his silk business to the town from neighbouring Pebmarsh in 1809. Eventually the firm he founded developed into an international combine, though, sadly, it has now left Braintree.

In 1834, just before the present railway was built from Witham, there were four licensed stage coaches passing through Braintree from London (40 miles) and Chelmsford (12 miles) to Bury St Edmunds and beyond. Overnight accommodation and a change of horses were provided there. There were also local coaches to Colchester (15 miles), Bishops Stortford, Clare, Hedingham and Yeldham, as well as regular carrier services to London, Colchester, Chelmsford, and Bishops Stortford. All enhanced the town's trade. The railway was originally built with a double track to Maldon and it was envisaged that much of its traffic would be to and from the then thriving port, so connecting the town to extensive sea-borne trade, replacing the old turnpike which entered the town via Notley Road. However, after a short period one track was removed and the line developed as a branch, connecting to the Liverpool Street to Norwich main line, although for a time there was also a more modest connection through to Dunmow and Bishops Stortford.

The growth and prosperity of the weaving and silk industry, together with the later establishment of rapidly expanding engineering firms, like Crittall Windows and Lake & Elliot, which between them produced a remarkably wide range of technically advanced industrial products, resulted in a steady increase in the population of the town. In 1849 it comprised some 4,000 people and a hundred years later, in 1951, it had risen to 17,520. By then there were already substantial numbers of workers commuting between the neighbouring towns of Chelmsford, Braintree, Halstead, Witham and Maldon to the different factories. Many Braintree people were employed in the then thriving Marconi, Crompton and Hoffmann factories at Chelmsford, mostly travelling to and fro by Hicks buses.

Today the original street pattern established by the Bishop of London, over 800 years ago, still substantially survives as the present town centre, although over the centuries the buildings facing High Street, Bank Street and Great Square have been mostly rebuilt several times. However, many of considerable age still remain. In 1993 much was pedestrianised but, sadly, the once important livestock market, originally held in the Great Square, High Street and Bank Street and latterly in covered premises on the present site of Tesco, has gone. All that remains of Braintree's former importance as a market town are the thriving retail stalls in the town centre. Sadly, too, the important landmarks of the Corn Exchange and the Horn Hotel have also disappeared, though the structure of the latter remains. Nevertheless, the town retains the legacy of numerous gifts received from Courtauld's.

Braintree and Bocking played their full part in both world wars, with most of the factories turning to war production. Crittall's, in particular, had a vital role making munitions. In the Second World War it also manufactured important items such as Bailey bridge parts, enabling the Allies to speedily replace destroyed bridges which would otherwise have hindered their advance. The town was also a target for enemy aircraft. In the First World War it was bombed several times by Zeppelins and in the Second by the Luftwaffe, as well as V1s and V2s. Many wartime airfields were constructed in the vicinity and the town was much frequented by off-duty US airmen; an American military hospital also existed nearby.

Following the closure of many of its main industries Braintree entered into a period of decline during the second half of the last century. However, more recently the town's fortunes have seen a remarkable recovery, with substantial new and attractive residential development taking place around its expanding perimeter. Much of this has been due to the electrification of the branch railway, which provides a connection to the main line at Witham giving fast passenger services to London and to the improved road links to London and elsewhere via the A12 and the M11, all of which encourage commuters to the town. Today, new bypasses almost encircle the town. Braintree's relative proximity to Stansted Airport, with its substantial employment possibilities, also increases its attractiveness. Occupying part of the old industrial area is a massive new out-of-town shopping centre known as Freeport, which has captured a large slice of retail trade, while other abandoned industrial and railway land has been redeveloped for residential purposes.

In the 1970s, as a result of major national local government changes, the Urban District of Braintree and Bocking lost its cherished independence and became incorporated within a considerably larger authority – the Braintree District Council – which now covers a wide area of north Essex, reaching from the fringes of Chelmsford Borough at Ford End, to the River Stour and the Suffolk communities of Sudbury and Bures, encompassing a substantial area of attractive countryside, together with the smaller towns of Witham and Halstead.

ACKNOWLEDGEMENTS & BIBLIOGRAPHY

The photographs appear by kind permission of the following:

Mr W. Bateman, Braintree and Bocking Heritage Trust, Crittall Windows Ltd, Mrs R. Goodwin, Mr Joscelyne, Mr G.R. Mortimer. Others came from the author's own collection.

I also acknowledge the help given by my wife, Marion, who cheerfully corrected the grammatical and spelling errors and made many invaluable suggestions on the content.

Braintree and Bocking, J. & S. Adlam & M. Charlton (1995).
Braintree & Bocking – A Pictorial History, John Marriage (1994)
Braintree and Bocking in Old Postcards Vols I, II & III, D. Brisley (1988)
Braintree & Bocking, M. Baker (1981)
Buildings of England: Essex, N. Pevsner (1954)
Some Essex Water Mills, Hervey Benham (1976)
Window Vision, D.J. Blake (1989)

1

Town Centre

The George Yard shopping precinct, 2003.

Great Square, *c.* 1900. Despite its name, the square is not large but, nevertheless, stands in a pivotal position between the High Street, the main shopping and trading centre and the important market area. Dominating is the Great House, a brick-fronted timber-framed building partially occupied by the Constitutional Club. It is viewed here from High Street.

Today the square remains an important link between High Street and the former market area. Sadly, it is now only occupied by retail stalls, but even so it is normally busy with people.

Great Square, looking towards High Street, *c.* 1900. It is flanked on the left side by elegant Georgian buildings, several in private occupation, and on the right by smaller shops and a public house.

As a result of traffic measures Great Square is no longer a through route for vehicular traffic and trees have softened its appearance. On the left the former house has been replaced by a modern Georgian-style office block.

George Yard as it appeared in 1900, when it had only a narrow entrance from Bank Street via a 'gant' (alleyway). Francis Crittall started his engineering business in the buildings on the right, eventually encroaching on to the alleyway, before moving to a purpose-built factory in Manor Street.

Today, the same buildings have been refurbished and incorporated within the present well-laid-out and attractive George Yard shopping precinct, which has a widened entrance from Bank Street.

In 1910 New Street was one of the busiest and most notorious streets in the town. A hundred years ago there were three pubs near its junction with Great Square – the Three Tuns, the George and the Green Man, respectively known as 'Little Hell', 'Great Hell' and 'Damnation'! All were eventually incorporated into Joscelyne's furniture store.

New Street is now a smart pedestrian route, and most of the buildings seen in the upper picture have been renovated or replaced by others in a similar style.

High Street, looking towards Chelmsford on a Wednesday market day, 1903. A herd of sheep is being driven towards the market and various goods are laid out for inspection in the road. The Horn Hotel, once a coaching inn, is on the left, while beyond is the Corn Exchange, with its useful clock.

In recent years the road has been narrowed and converted to one way, making it safer for pedestrians. Sadly the Horn Hotel is now used for retail purposes while the Corn Exchange has been demolished, though happily the clock has been transferred to the replacement building.

Looking up High Street towards the Bank Street/Great Square junction, market day, *c.* 1900. On the right is the Corn Exchange, built in 1839, with its clock mounted at first-floor level.

This picture of almost the same place in about 1920 shows a changing scene. The shoe shop at the corner of Bank Street and Great Square, facing the camera, has been replaced by a new two-storey building occupied by Foster Brothers, men's and boys' outfitters. The corner became known as Foster's Corner.

The Corn Exchange was demolished in the 1960s and replaced by a less interesting building. However, owing to public demand, the clock was refitted and remains a prominent feature. Today Foster's premises are occupied by a bank. The road has been narrowed and made one way, allowing more pavement space for pedestrians and attractive street furniture.

A quiet sunny day in the High Street, looking towards Chelmsford, with a few people about, *c.* 1900. A dog looks curiously at the photographer.

A hundred years later. Most of the buildings seen in the picture on the left remain, though changes have taken place at ground-floor level with a variety of shopping outlets. It remains a well-patronised street.

The southern side of High Street at its junction with Bank Street and Great Square, looking towards Chelmsford on a quiet day, *c.* 1900. In the centre of the picture is the Horn Hotel, with the Corn Exchange two doors away.

Seen here, over a hundred years later, most of the buildings remain and have clearly been smartened up – a sure sign of the current prosperity of the town. Today retail predominates.

Gibson's shop at 71 High Street, *c.* 1900. it carried a substantial stock of watches, jewellery and fancy goods. Outside, three ornate hanging gas lamps light the display.

Over a hundred years later the shop is still a jeweller's and little change has taken place to the front except for the fascia, now graced with the name of R.G. Swain. Sadly, though, the lamps have gone. Modern interior and street lighting have made them obsolete.

The Central Cinema, seen here in 1928, was once a mecca for film buffs and one of two cinemas in the town. The film being shown was *The Eagle*, the hit of the year, starring the dashingly handsome screen idol of the time, Rudolph Valentino.

The same building is now occupied by Townrow, the Braintree departmental store, though after closure as a cinema it was for a time occupied by Tesco, who later moved to purpose-built premises in the Market Place.

Joscelyne's furnishers and house removals, *c.* 1900. This was one of the departmental stores in the town, where customers were invited to browse. It occupied premises at the corner of High Street and New Street and held large stocks of furniture and household goods.

After the closure of Joscelyne's the premises were rebuilt to similar dimensions. They remain in retail use.

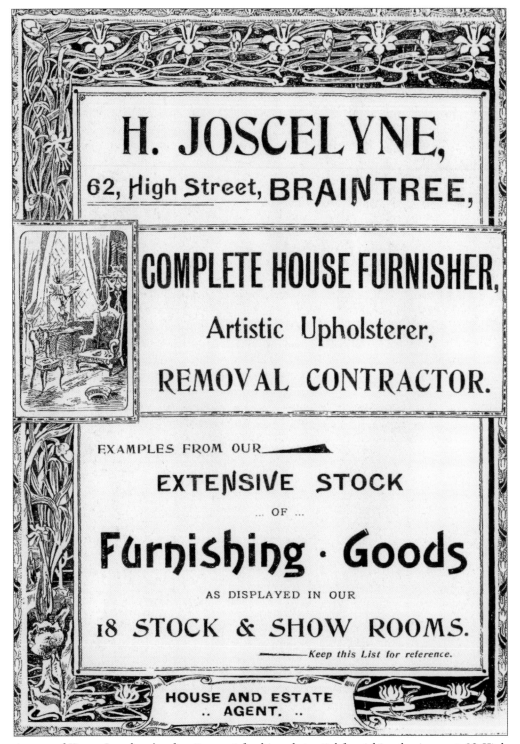

A copy of Henry Joscelyne's advertisement for his substantial furnishing business at 62 High Street, *c.* 1900.

Bank Street, looking towards the White Hart junction, *c.* 1900. In those days it was very narrow along its entire length, but was later widened by the acquisition of a strangely sited island garden in the road and various other properties, some demolished as a result of war damage.

The same view today, now converted to a pedestrian route. On the left a narrow gant or alleyway has been widened to form an impressive tunnel entrance to the George Yard shopping precinct, through the attractive two-storey brick-fronted Georgian building standing at the entrance to Bank Street.

James Bowtell's high-class family grocery in Bank Street, *c.* 1925. In later years it was reduced to a single unit, and it closed in 1994.

The premises are now occupied in part by a charity shop and by a florist. However, apart from new blinds there has been little change to the shopfront.

Bank Street seen from the White Hart junction, 1900. The broad area in front of the timber-framed building in the distance was formed by incorporating a garden into the highway. Previously the road passed either side, creating a leafy island. Immediately on the right is the former Sparrow Tufnell Bank, also known as the Essex Bank.

As a result of the demolition of properties on the left side the street has been further widened, with new post-war building set back from the original alignment. In more recent times new tree planting has taken place within the curtilage of the street and traffic has been restricted. On the right Barclays, successor to the Essex Bank, still occupies the corner premises.

A closer look at the lower part of Bank Street, *c.* 1938. In those days there was complete freedom for vehicles and pedestrians to pass. There was a tight squeeze at the narrow section, though, particularly for buses.

Although the building facing the camera has changed little, the pre-war occupiers have now moved to nearby High Street and other retail suppliers now possess the premises.

On 16 February 1941 Braintree suffered a night raid when several bombs were dropped on the town. One fell in Bank Street destroying Lloyds Bank and adjacent shops. This picture was taken soon after the debris was removed.

Redevelopment took place after the war: the new buildings were set back so that the road could be widened. Like so much redevelopment of the time this was of a design not really in keeping with the traditional appearance of the town.

Some months after the debris was removed from the Bank Street site Lloyds Bank erected a small temporary pre-cast concrete hut from which they conducted their business for a number of years.

In early post-war years redevelopment of the bombed site took place, including, at the corner of Rayne Road, a new branch of Lloyds Bank.

St Michael's Church, High Street, *c.* 1938. There is just a glimpse of the fountain designed by the sculptor John Hodge and donated to the town by Sir W.J. Courtauld in memory of King George V. A particular feature of the church is its tall shingled broach spire.

Little change has taken place subsequently to either the church or the fountain. However, the once busy area is today somewhat isolated because of shifting road patterns.

The fountain, a few years after construction in July 1937. In the centre a youth holds a fish in each hand, while aquatic animals arch water into the pool basin.

Unfortunately this attractive feature is now rather neglected and forlorn, barely raising any interest from the few passers-by, a sad comment on an otherwise thriving town.

A further view of the fountain, *c.* 1980. The photographer is looking towards the Church Street/ High Street junction, the nursing home built by Sir W.J. Courtauld and the Fountain Inn.

Church Street has subsequently become an important traffic route, with a major junction at London Road and High Street. The inn has now become the H_2O, a much less charming title.

St Michael's Church from Church Street, *c.* 1900. It is thought that some parts of the church date back to the twelfth or thirteenth centuries, and contain Roman bricks. It has been suggested that the Romans may have had a military camp in the vicinity.

Although there have been few changes to the church itself, the surroundings have been transformed by the removal of the tombstones to create a lawn. While this action has undoubtedly improved the surroundings, it has also eliminated some of the town's history.

The once busy Orange Tree Inn in the Market Place, *c.* 1905. Spectators idle by the livestock pens to view the stock and exchange gossip.

The inn was demolished in 1957 and replaced by a modern building of similar size, most of which is now occupied by an insurance broker, though its name survives on a small part of the building. The site of the stock pens has become a parking area.

Market Place, *c.* 1900. In its prime Braintree market was always bustling with activity. Sheep, cattle and horses were for sale, merchandise was sold and deals were struck amid the general hubbub. In the distance is Balls & Balls' Cattle Market.

The former cattle market was replaced by a branch of Tesco, which moved in the 1960s from premises in the High Street. Parked cars now replace the pens.

A sunny market day, *c.* 1900, looking across the Market Square towards Great Square, busy with stalls and shoppers. On the right is the Nags Head. On the drinking fountain presented by George Courtauld in 1882 is inscribed the following: 'He sendeth the springs into the valley which run among the hills That ye may drink, both ye and your cattle and your beasts.'

Today the Square is a quieter place, mainly given over to the motor car and with only a few stalls on market days. The public house is now known as the Globe.

A closer view of the drinking fountain, surmounted by a large ornate gas lamp, *c.* 1900. Then as now, it is the dominant feature in the square.

Today, much of its surroundings have been pedestrianised. The drinking trough has been replaced by a circular bench – a favourite meeting place for young people. Changes have also taken place to the head of the fountain. A globe-shaped lantern replaces the original and, rather strangely, a golden long eared owl, with prey, stands on top!

The Square looking towards Market Street, *c.* 1900. On the right are the former sheep pens, on land once known as Fairfield, and on the left is a glimpse of the Manor Street School.

Behind the fountain the two-storey premises are still shops, but the former school is now Braintree District Museum. On the right a corner of the former Town Hall, opened in 1928, is on the site of the old sheep pens. Marring the view, a somewhat utilitarian bus shelter has been placed close to the fountain.

A rear view of the Town Hall from Market Street as it appeared shortly after opening in 1928.

Little change has taken place to the building in the intervening time. It was fortunate that during the war years the ornate cast-iron railings surrounding the rear service area were not melted down for munitions.

Braintree Town Hall, *c.* 1935. This impressive neo-Georgian building was presented to the town by Sir W.J. Courtauld and was the heart of local administration for over forty years. It was built in 1926–8 and designed by Vincent Harris. A particular feature is the central open bell turret.

As a result of local government changes in 1974 Braintree and Bocking became part of a much larger authority, which required more space. Consequently new offices were built at The Causeway, and the old Town Hall became the tourist centre. To the right is the striking new public library, built in the early 1990s.

Hicks buses were once a familiar sight on the Braintree streets including this early vehicle, *c.* 1905. In the 1950s the company was taken over by the Eastern National Bus Company of Chelmsford, now part of First Bus.

A familiar sight today is this small bus, which has a similar passenger capacity to Hicks' original 1905 bus. It operates a limited service between the Market Square and the Freeport at Chapel Hill, taking a circular route round the town.

The interior of Manor Street School, *c.* 1905. The school was built in 1863, at George Courtauld's expense, to a design fairly typical of the time. Here, the teachers and an infants' class have been carefully positioned in one corner of the large classroom for the picture.

The school is now home to the Braintree District Museum and still echoes to the sounds of today's visiting children. The former classroom pictured above is now used as a display area.

In the days before heavy traffic the local hunt would meet for the ritual 'stirrup cup' outside the White Hart Hotel, pictured here in about 1905.

Today the old public house is at the heart of a busy urban area and the open countryside has receded a fair distance away. Considerable redevelopment has taken place in the vicinity of the old building, which has had its appearance changed by the removal of plasterwork, thus exposing the underlying timber and producing an aspect more akin to southern England than that of East Anglia.

The White Hart corner from Bank Street, looking towards Bocking End, *c.* 1905. For centuries the hotel (right) dominated the town when approaching from Rayne Road (Stane Street) The old Roman highway continues beyond the junction as Coggeshall Road. Its entrance is glimpsed between the shop and the public house.

In recent years through traffic has been removed from the town centre by the construction of a bypass and the junction is now of much less importance. In addition, the carriageway has been narrowed and, in part, made one way.

Bocking End, looking towards Convent Bridge, *c.* 1925. On the left is Braintree and West Essex Co-operative Society's main store, then only eight years old and a mecca for shoppers after their 'divi'.

Within the last few years the former Co-operative premises have been completely rebuilt and are now occupied by other tenants. The main Co-operative store is now in the George shopping precinct and, following amalgamation with the Chelmsford Star Co-operative Society, is now known as the Quadrant.

Coggeshall Road, looking towards the White Hart corner, *c.* 1960, shortly after reconstruction following war damage. Sadly, like so much development of the 1960s the buildings were to a design somewhat alien to their surroundings.

Some forty years later window boxes and tree planting have softened these post-war buildings. More happily, those in the distance that replaced the old Co-op have a more pleasing appearance, and are in scale with their surroundings.

The Braintree and Bocking Institute, *c.* 1905. It was founded as the Literary and Mechanics' Institute in 1845 but was rebuilt at a cost of £3,000 in 1863 following a bequest from George Courtauld. Over the years it has been used for a wide range of activities, from theatre groups to dog shows.

In recent years the building has been refurbished and the rather grandiose entrance gates removed. This has created a wide driveway, giving access for development and parking at the rear.

A close-up of the former Braintree and Bocking Co-operative Society's central stores at Bocking End, *c.* 1925, with its distinctive hexagonal clock tower and interesting dome.

Sadly, the clock tower has now gone. The replacement shopping terrace replicates, to some extent, the earlier building and even has the same number of gables.

Mr Bateman stands in the entrance to his general shoe shop at 12 Coggeshall Road in 1897. He was also a supplier of surgical boots.

Mr Bateman's former premises have now reverted to two shops, with little change to the fronts other than the paintwork.

2

The Environs

Coggeshall Road, looking towards the White Hart corner, *c.* 1900.

The County High School, Coggeshall Road, *c.* 1925. It was built by Essex County Council in 1907 on land given by Mrs Sydney Courtauld of Bocking Place. One of the first governors was Sir W. J. Courtauld JP.

Subsequently very little has changed, and the building is now used by the Essex County Council's social services department.

Coggeshall Road, looking east, *c.* 1910. On the left is the County Court built in 1852 at a cost of £3,000. A more recent use has been as the town's public library.

Within the last few years a new library has been built next to the former Town Hall in Fairfield Road, and the old County Court is now for sale. Much of the former library's surroundings are unchanged.

Coggeshall Road, looking towards the White Hart corner, *c.* 1910. On the left is a terrace of small timber-framed cottages, while on the opposite side there is a glimpse of the County Court. Next to it is Brigand Cottage, once occupied by the gamekeeper to a local celebrity, Dr Jack Harrison. The cottage was named after a lucky win on the horses.

Many of the buildings seen in the upper picture still survive, but the road is now much busier, despite the construction of a bypass in recent years. Traffic noise and fumes are now more of a problem to the people in the cottages.

The night air raid of 21 February 1941 saw Braintree Motor Garage completely destroyed, together with the unfortunate cars on the forecourt at the time. Also demolished was the adjacent manse.

The site is now part of Sainsbury's car park, which has been attractively landscaped with trees and shrubs.

The Coggeshall Road/Railway Street junction, *c.* 1910. On the corner is the Fox and Hounds pub, demolished in the 1960s for road improvements.

Residential development is currently taking place on the site of the public house, together with adjoining land, but the wide gabled building on the far side of Railway Street survives.

The Congregational church, London Road, was built in 1832 at a cost of £1,400 in what was then a quiet and peaceful road. It replaced a building that once stood on land now part of the George Yard shopping precinct.

Today the church – now the United Reform Church – is sited close to the insensitively designed junction with Pierrefitte Way, and its quiet ambience is shattered for ever.

Set back from London Road and opposite the church, this terrace of roomy semi-detached Edwardian middle-class houses was built during the early part of the last century, when they would have been extremely desirable properties.

One or two of the houses have been removed to make way for the junction with Pierrefitte Way. Traffic frequently has to queue at busy times of the day outside the properties, making exit difficult, and damaging the environment with noise and fumes.

Another view of London Road, looking from just beyond the now derelict Dunmow railway line towards Chelmsford, c. 1900.

The same view now. Most of the houses still survive, albeit with their front gardens converted into parking for the owners' cars.

The site of the William Julian Courtauld Cottage Hospital in London Road, just prior to its construction when the land was still in agricultural use. The hospital opened in 1921, with four wards, but was later extended.

The hospital is now used primarily for maternity care, with accident and emergency cases dealt with at Broomfield Hospital, Chelmsford.

Lyton, London Road, built by Francis Crittall, *c.* 1905. The house includes the then quite revolutionary metal window frames he designed.

Major changes have since taken place to the property, and a modern house has been built alongside.

The entrance to the cemetery in London Road, *c.* 1910. The chapel, behind the avenue of trees, was built in the Gothic revival style, as were the gate piers.

In recent years the gatehouse has been completely rebuilt, together with the gates. The maturing trees have softened its rather severe appearance.

n this picture of about 1920, Grenville Road appears deceptively quiet. However, with the growth of motor raffic it became a busy short cut linking London Road with Rayne Road, for vehicles wishing to avoid High treet and Bank Street.

Vith the construction of Pierrefitte Way in 1988 the road became a quiet cul-de-sac, and some measure of eace was restored to the residents.

Twyford House, Rayne Road, *c*. 1895. This was a beautiful Georgian town mansion, which dominated the road near the White Hart. It is reputed that John Bunyan stayed there. More recently the electricity board took over the building and crudely inserted a shopfront at ground-floor level. When George Yard opened the board moved there.

After a period of uncertainty, when the premises were unused and seemed in danger of demolition, a ground-floor shop selling fabrics opened. The future of the building now seems more secure.

St Michael's Hospital, Rayne Road, *c.* 1905. At the time of the photograph this was the Braintree Union Workhouse, a rather grim-looking building where many destitute working-class people would, unfortunately, end their days.

Since those times the building has been taken over by the National Health Service and it now deals far more sympathetically with the elderly. Many changes have taken place both internally and externally, creating a more welcoming atmosphere.

Rayne Road, looking away from the White Hart corner, *c.* 1905, with only a horse and cart occupying the centre of the road.

When this picture was taken one Sunday the road was quiet, but on weekdays the road is much used. Delays frequently occur leading up to the traffic lights at the White Hart corner – a far cry from the peace of yesteryear. Sadly, the attractive double-fronted timber-framed building on the right-hand side of the upper picture has now disappeared.

Rayne Road, looking towards the White Hart junction, *c.* 1910. The Victorian Gothic structure is the Methodist church, opened in 1868. Built to accommodate a congregation of 450, it had a manse and Sunday school adjoining. Twyford House can be seen in the distance.

The church was demolished in 1988 to make way for the George Yard shopping precinct, while the school and manse were removed in 1937 to allow Braintree Co-operative Society to extend their premises. By happy chance – or design – the present tower within the scheme echoes, to some extent, the church tower, and provides a welcome feature along this part of the road.

At the turn of the nineteenth to twentieth century these timber-framed and plaster cottages in Rayne Road faced undeveloped land on the town's edge. It is thought that they were originally occupied by silk out-workers, and the south-facing windows would have provided good light.

Now these houses are in the heart of Braintree, where they remain an attractive feature. Sadly, however, the wrought-iron boundary fences have gone, presumably the result of wartime scrap collection. Parking of cars in some of the front gardens has further marred their appearance.

Another view of Rayne Road, looking towards the White Hart corner, *c.* 1905. On the left are the silk weavers' cottages, seen in the earlier picture, faced by newly built Victorian terraced houses.

n 1988 Pierrefitte Way was built, creating a major junction with Rayne Road and sweeping away several of he terraced houses seen in the picture above.

This charming scene shows the road crossing Pods Brook via a humpbacked bridge on the way to Rayne village, *c.* 1905. In those days its surroundings were completely rural and very little traffic disturbed the tranquillity.

Now the road is urbanised, complete with pavements, yellow lines and traffic islands. The humpbacked bridge has been levelled and the locality is now on the fringe of town and has lost its rural charm.

The Sun Lido was a privately owned open air swimming pool in Rayne Road, and was a very popular amenity in the 1920s. It was a big disappointment to Braintree residents when it closed in the 1950s.

The site is now occupied by a newly built housing estate, whose central square displays this attractive sign.

Immediately next to the Sun Lido swimming pool was another popular feature – the Sun Lido boating lake. Sadly, this also closed in the 1950s.

Today the boating lake is open land, and only a small stream running through it is a reminder of its former existence.

Before the railway came Notley Road was one of the busiest entrances into the town, and a turnpike carrying goods to and from the east coast port of Maldon. By about 1910 it had become a quiet lane flanked by artisans' cottages.

Few changes have taken place to the adjacent properties but this road is now a serious bottleneck in today's heavy traffic.

A short distance towards Notley the road crosses the River Brain via Hoppit Bridge. In the early part of the last century the bridge was narrow and humpbacked, fringed by willows.

In subsequent years both the bridge and the road have been widened, and the hump levelled. Houses stand on the former meadows, and the river is confined to a narrow channel.

For much of the year the River Brain is only a small stream, but after heavy rain the road was liable to flood. A board walk was provided for pedestrian use but horse-drawn traffic had to traverse the swollen waters. Here, a summer flood attracts local children, *c.* 1910.

As a result of road level changes floods are now a thing of the past, but the country picture is lost forever under concrete.

Station Approach, *c.* 1910. At this time the land on the north side was in use as a railway goods yard. A spur track crossed the road and connected to the Dunmow line east of the station.

Pleasant modern terraced houses now occupy the site, giving their owners convenient access to the railway station on the opposite side of the road.

The exterior of Braintree railway station, *c.* 1905. This station replaced the original 1848 building when the line was extended to Dunmow and Bishops Stortford.

Following the closure of the line between Braintree and Bishops Stortford this station became the terminus. It remains busy with frequent electric train services to Witham and London.

The railway station looking towards Witham, *c.* 1910. A double track existed at the various stations to allow trains to pass, but elsewhere it was single. The iron Victorian footbridge connected the two platforms.

Little change has taken place to the town side of the station, although when the second track was removed in the 1950s, the buildings on the far side and the footbridge were removed.

EASTERN COUNTIES' RAILWAY.

CHEAP TRIP
TO
LONDON.

On MONDAY, Aug. 13th, 1860,

JOHNSON'S
FIRST SPECIAL
EXCURSION TRAIN,
FOR THE SEASON,

Will leave Braintree Station at 6.30 a.m. calling at Witham at 6.50. a.m., returning from Bishopsgate Station at 8 p.m.

Giving ELEVEN HOURS IN LONDON.

FARES THERE & BACK.

FIRST CLASS.   COVERED CARRIAGES

5s.   2s.6d.

Children under 12 years of age half-price.

TICKETS may be had up to Saturday, the 11th Inst. of Mr. Finney, Bocking; Mr. Joseph Godfrey Downing, Chemist, Mr. Fred. Andrews, Grocer, and Mr. I. Clayden, Railway Tavern, Braintree; and Railway Stations, Witham and Braintree.

Any further Information may be had of the Contractor

Wm. JOHNSON, Railway Coal Depot.

The opening of the railways in 1848 quickly created a demand by the general public for cheap travel, and by 1860 enterprising local businessmen had seen the possibility of profitable day excursions to London.

Braintree's first railway station, built in 1849, was the terminus of the line from Witham and Maldon. The small building comprised a waiting room, a booking office and storage area. Passengers went to the platform through the building set at right angles. It was replaced in 1889 by the present station but much of the area behind stayed in railway use. For many years it was used as the office of a builder's merchant. This photograph was taken in 1993 prior to demolition.

A large estate has now replaced the former siding and these three-storey town houses stand on the site of the former station.

The engine shed, pictured here in 1993, was near the original railway station, close to the junction of Railway Street and Rose Hill.

A terrace of three-storey town houses has now replaced the old shed. The tower block marks the junction of Railway Street with Rose Hill.

The junction of Railway Street and South Street, *c.* 2000. The demolition of the former goods yard premises on the right-hand side of the picture is in progress.

The 2003 development on this brownfield site is in a style which contrasts sharply with the old part of the town, totally transforming the locality. It has brought in many newcomers, and has cleared up a blighted area.

The former Warner Silk factory at New Mills (left), South Street, *c.* 1910. It was built over 160 years ago by Daniel Walters and later taken over by Warners, who closed the factory in 1971.

Part of the old factory reopened some years ago as a working silk museum, and is the sole reminder of an industry that once dominated the life and economy of Braintree.

South Street, *c.* 1910. The view looks towards Railway Street from Station Approach, whose entrance is marked by a brick pier with an inset post office box and a gas lamp standard. Somewhat unusually for the style of properties, they are set well back from the road.

Although seemingly traffic-free in this picture, South Street is an increasingly busy through road, a role which it seems destined to continue as a result of the high density housing that is being built to the east. As with so many properties today the front gardens are now used for off street parking.

An attractive terrace of thatched cottages in Cressing Road, *c.* 1910. Originally the cottages were surrounded by open countryside but now they are somewhat incongruously surrounded by newer houses.

In recent years the terrace has been lovingly converted into a single house with a large central dormer and entrance, while at one side a former living room has been converted into a garage.

The Avenue, *c.* 1915, when it was one of the more fashionable places to live. Substantially built Victorian houses overlooked the arboreal grounds of Mount House.

The road still has a quiet and peaceful ambience. Sadly, though, the street trees seen in the upper picture have been badly mutilated over the years, with side branches being lopped away each year.

Another view of The Avenue, from Coggeshall Road, *c.* 1915. The houses along this part of the road have their privacy protected by a substantial brick wall.

Apart from the mutilation of the street trees little has changed in the intervening years, other than the arrival of a pillar box.

Manor Street, looking eastwards towards Railway Street, *c*. 1910. On the left is the gate to Manor Street School. In its day the school achieved good scholastic results, particularly in the three Rs, which was helped by strong classroom and parental discipline.

Nowadays the school buildings are completely outmoded and children's education is carried on elsewhere. Nevertheless, the old building continues in useful service as a museum.

In the late 1980s the parent company of Crittall's decided that its factories in Braintree and Witham had become antiquated and should be replaced with a state of the art factory in Springwood Drive. On its completion the existing factories were closed, and the Council agreed to their sites being redeveloped for residential purposes. This picture shows the works in Manor Street shortly after closure in the 1990s.

The same site in 2003. This unusual landmark residential tower block has now replaced the old factory.

Crittall's had a history of encouraging sport and social recreation, and their club in Coggeshall Road was immensely popular with their staff and others. This picture was taken in 1993 soon after it had closed. It has been replaced by new premises in Springwood Drive.

Only the continued existence of several distinctive older semi-detached houses enables this site to be identified, as there is little to mark the former club, which has been replaced by modern houses.

A view of part of Crittall's Manor Works, looking towards the Railway Street junction soon after the closure of the factory, *c.* 1993.

All trace of the factory has now disappeared and it has been replaced by a new housing estate.

CRITTALL WINDOWS

FOR THE NEW HOUSES

By specifying STANDARD metal windows—
from British Standard 990 : 1945 — you help to
reduce the present unavoidable delay in delivery,
and at the same time you ensure highest
quality and lowest cost. Ask for leaflet 115 B.

THE CRITTALL MANUFACTURING CO. LTD.
BRAINTREE, ENGLAND

One of Crittall's early post-war advertisements. The firm regularly employed Ernest Howard Shepard, illustrator of A.A. Milne's *Christopher Robin* and *Winnie the Pooh* books, and his style certainly shows here.

Victoria Street, *c.* 1910. On the right is a row of prosperous late Victorian semi-detached villas, with regular bay windows, complete with stone mullions and arched door entrances. Their front boundaries are marked by ornate ironwork. On the left is a glimpse of open land forming part of the Fairfield, and behind the trees is the Territorial Army Drill Hall.

The street is now one way, taking traffic from the town centre. The houses are little changed except for the loss of the iron railings. On the left there is now a large car and bus park, while the drill hall is now a community centre.

Courtauld's Braintree Mill, Chapel Hill, *c.* 1915. In the foreground is the former mill race of the River Brain. This once supplied water power to the silk mill and also provided a rustic setting at the same time, unusual for a working mill of the era.

Sadly, Courtauld's completely withdrew from the town in 1985, causing huge redundancies, and the factory was demolished soon after. It is now difficult to pinpoint the exact site of the above scene. However, the Council has erected an interpretative board nearby providing an outline history.

The Causeway, *c.* 1905. On the right is the former British School founded by the adjoining Congregational church. The school was built in 1852 and accommodated up to 350 boys and girls. It replaced an earlier one which opened in the mid-eighteenth century with a roll of some thirty pupils.

In 1979, after being disused for many years, the school was demolished and replaced by offices for the newly created Braintree District Council. The new building was named, unsurprisingly, Causeway House.

The entrance to Braintree and Bocking Public Gardens at The Causeway, *c.* 1910. Encompassing 5½ acres, they were once part of the grounds of Mrs George Courtauld's garden. On the left is the lodge house, built just prior to the opening of the gardens in 1888.

The entrance has changed little, except that brick pillars have replaced the former wrought-iron entrance posts. The gardens remain extremely popular. The rapidly increasing housing area surrounding the park means it is now of even greater amenity value than in the last century. In recognition of this the park has recently received grants from lottery funds.

The gardens, looking towards the entrance, *c.* 1910. Then, as now, they were popular with young mothers and their children.

The scene has changed little over the last century. The well-tended park remains a credit to the local council.

The circular ornamental water feature in the public garden, *c.* 1910, complete with its attractive fountain.

The pond continues to draw children and adults alike but, sadly, like all the other fountains in the town there is no flowing water.

One of the original features of the gardens was the tennis courts, seen here in about 1910. Then, as now, tennis was a popular sport with children and adults alike.

Lush vegetation surrounds the same courts photographed on a quiet weekday afternoon in summer 2003, before the evening rush to play.

An unusual feature in the gardens was the thatched bandstand. This was regularly used in Victorian times for Sunday afternoon brass band concerts.

Despite the high maintenance costs the bandstand has survived, and continues to play host to local musicians who give popular summer concerts. As can be seen, the original park benches also remain.

Like most communities the town suffered the
loss of many of its citizens during the First
World War. This memorial was erected a few
years after the end of hostilities in the gardens
next to The Causeway.

Some eighty years later the stark
appearance of the monument has softened
with the growth of surrounding tree cover.

Bocking Place, built in 1888 and set in 10 acres of land, was originally the home of Sidney Courtauld. In 1922 it became the Braintree Intermediate School, the first school of its kind in Essex. Its aim was to provide a level of education between that of local senior schools and grammar schools, but it was incorporated into the High School in 1938. It is seen here across the extensive grounds, *c.* 1925.

This handsome Victorian building has recently been converted into flats, while much of the grounds are now open to the public.

A closer view of Bocking Place from the entrance drive, in about 1925. The headmaster of the Intermediate School for the whole of its existence was G.A. Birnage BSc.

Externally few changes have taken place. New houses have been built to the west of the house on part of the grounds.

Coronation Road, a turning off Notley Road, is seen here in about 1910, a few years after the properties were built, following the accession to the throne of King Edward VII.

At the turn of the century only very wealthy people had motor cars and it would have been unthinkable for these houses to have had garages. Today's residents' vastly improved standard of living is reflected in the almost continuous street parking.

3

Bocking

Bradford Street – unquestionably the most attractive road in Braintree and Bocking.

St Peter's Church, in a quiet side road off The Causeway, is an attractive Victorian church built in 1897 by the architect Micklethwaite. It is pictured here a few years later.

Over the hundred or so intervening years there have been few outward changes, other than the growth of adjacent trees and shrubs to create a more established appearance.

Immediately opposite the church is the
entrance to St Peter's Walk, a leafy footpath
leading to the town centre and in earlier times
a popular lovers' walk.

The walk remains tree lined and is now a
busy shortcut. It is now less isolated, as on
one side there are playing fields and at one
point it is bisected by an entrance drive
leading to an educational establishment.

Looking northwards along Bradford Street, from near its junction with The Causeway, *c.* 1905. In those days many prosperous weavers and business people had property there. Immediately on the left is The Old House, once the home of a wool merchant.

Today, much of the street is within an Outstanding Conservation Area, though, sadly, for most of the day its appearance is marred by the presence of through traffic, creating dust, noise and disturbance.

Bradford Street, *c.* 1905. Its many large medieval timber-framed houses and shops of great character front the road as it winds down the hill towards the River Blackwater. Over their extended period of existence many of the properties have been refronted in brick and/or plaster to present a more classical appearance.

As a result of post-war planning legislation many of the buildings are listed and lovingly maintained by their owners. However, owing to the rise of supermarkets many of the small shops interspersing the houses have been converted into private residences.

A closer look at the lower end of Bradford Street, *c.* 1900. The old Woolpack Inn is an attractive sixteenth-century structure. Gables at three different levels project beyond the first-floor overhang. It has a curved bressummer (a large beam supporting the front of the building) dated 1590. Further away from the camera is the fourteenth-century Wentworth House, again with three gables.

Little physical change has taken place to the various buildings, though many now have a much smarter appearance – the result of current prosperity and the application of modern paints and colour wash. The prominent road markings in such a sensitive area are unfortunate.

Approaching the Six Bells corner, *c.* 1905. The gable of the public house with its overhanging sign can just be glimpsed behind the cottages on the left. On the right is Tudor House, with its overhanging upper storey dating back to the sixteenth century.

In more recent times the corner with Church Street has been widened and both the cottages and the Six Bells have gone. A modern building now occupies the corner site opposite where the pub stood.

The lower end of Bradford Street, *c.* 1920. It is flanked by smaller workers' cottages. As traffic was then very light it is surprising that a pavement is under construction, as evidenced by the wheelbarrow, hand roller and a heap of tarmac.

Many of the cottages on the left have been removed and there is now a small car park, but on the right few changes have occurred.

A wooden bridge spans the River Blackwater allowing travellers to proceed towards High Garrett along Broad Road, *c.* 1910. Before the bridge was built a ford existed on the spot. Beyond is the Fulling Mill House and the Franciscan Convent chapel, built in 1899.

By 1927 the wooden bridge had become seriously weakened and Essex County Council replaced it with the present steel and stone structure on the same alignment.

A summer's day in Church Lane looking towards Deanery corner, *c.* 1910. There is little movement along the road, apart from a man pushing a handcart.

It is now a busy traffic route and, on another hot sunny day in 2003, the photographer had to wait patiently for a gap in the traffic to get this shot. On the right is the goods entrance to Braintree College.

Bocking Mill, *c.* 1910. This beautiful white weather-boarded structure was built in 1580 and throughout its history has had a chequered career, having been used both for fulling and flour milling. As with most mills in Essex the water wheel was undershot, supplied by a drop of 6 ft. The mill pond is below. A ford passed through before the construction of the adjacent bridge.

The mill is now disused, although externally it is in immaculate condition. In its final working days the machinery was electrically operated and animal feed was produced.

Bocking Bridge, *c.* 1900. This was a sturdy wooden bridge built next to the original ford over the River Blackwater. To judge from its appearance the latter still seemed to be in regular use, albeit possibly to water the horses using the road.

In 1914, Kings Bridge was built on the site of the old ford, in commemoration of the reign of King Edward VII and the coronation of George V. Brick built, it is still in use today. The alignment of the wooden bridge is marked by the row of trees to the right.

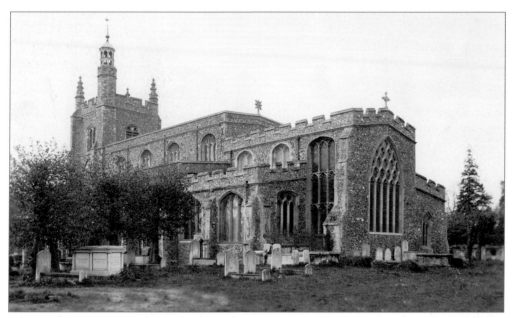

St Mary's Church, Bocking, *c.* 1910. Pevsner's description is of 'a large church for a prosperous village'. It was built in the fourteenth and fifteenth centuries with unusual diagonal buttresses, so broad that they have their own little buttresses. When the picture was taken the stair turret was surmounted by an attractive wooden cupola, added in 1887.

In recent years the various memorials have been removed and placed round the edges of the graveyard, thereby creating a lawn. While this is visually attractive, it is unfortunate that it destroys much local history. The cupola has also disappeared, as have the four ornamental pinnacles surmounting the buttresses.

The Workmen's Hall, *c.* 1905 (centre). This was built in 1884 for the benefit of factory employees. George Sherrin was the architect, who designed many other local buildings. To the left is the mainly three-storey Courtauld Bocking Silk weaving factory, with the old Royal pub in front. The pub was later demolished and the factory extended.

The former Workmen's Hall is now the church hall. The factory has gone and the site is empty. Mature trees now partially obscure a view of the church.

The Royal Almshouses were originally created in 1440 to provide accommodation for the local poor. They were rebuilt in 1869. In the foreground children play on the grass next to the Workmen's Hall.

A mature tree shelters the spot where the children were at play, but there is little change in appearance to either the former Workmen's Hall and the almshouses in the distance.

Looking up Church Street from the green, *c.* 1900. Set back and on the right is the Black Boy pub. Next but one to the house with dormer windows is the local branch of the Braintree and West Essex Co-operative Society, which opened its doors in 1880.

The Black Boy, like so many public houses in the area, has long gone. However, the Co-op remains, though rebuilt in 1913. Although not a problem a hundred years ago, today the long, climbing village street causes traffic difficulties, exacerbated by the many parked cars.

Church Street, looking downhill along the narrow village street towards the River Blackwater (Pant), *c.* 1910. Next to the telegraph pole in the centre of the picture is the water pump that once served this part of the community. Immediately on the right is the terrace of houses built at the turn of the nineteenth century.

The essential village character of the street still survives although some changes have occurred. In particular, infilling has been allowed at the far end of the terrace houses and the cottage nearest the camera has gone, replaced by a modern house.

The Co-op, built as part of an expansion by the society in Braintree, is halfway up Church Street. Next to it, and nearer the camera, is a small butcher's shop, one of several in the village.

The same scene today. The Co-op is now one of only a few shops left in Church Street. Many of the original houses have been replaced but the flint wall on the left remains. The street now boasts pavements on either side, albeit rather narrow.

These attractive cottages with dormer windows were at the top end of Church Street with little space between them and the road. In 1900, when this photograph was taken, no pavements existed.

The same corner today. Few of the original buildings still remain but pavements have been built to protect pedestrians from traffic.

These attractive lime-washed thatched cottages, seen here in about 1920, were set at right angles to the road next to the United Reform church.

Post-war Council-built bungalows are now on the site.

n 1872 Courtaulds built this row of workmen's cottages towards the top end of Church Street. They were ubstantial and attractively constructed to a standard well in advance of the times. An employee, Tam Vhybrow, watches the photographer with interest, as does the girl opposite, *c.* 1910.

he same properties today.

Bocking windmill, then a working post mill, *c.* 1910. It was originally sited further down hill, but when acquired by John Tabor, in 1829, it was moved to its present position and set on a round brick base.

The mill later fell into disuse, but in 1994 it was substantially restored to its original appearance and is the only Grade I listed windmill in Essex. It is now closely hemmed in by modern houses and approached by a small alley, but is open to the public.

The Deanery, Church Lane, *c.* 1900. It was originally a timber-framed building of medieval origin, standing in large grounds, but was later clad in brick and partly rendered, giving it a Victorian appearance. Dean Dr Christopher Wordsworth, the younger brother of the poet William Wordsworth, lived here from 1808 to 1815.

At the time of writing it is being converted into a residential care home.